COLLINS
COBUILD
ENGLISH
DICTIONARY
WORKBOOK

Malcolm Goodale

THE UNIVERSITY
OF BIRMINGHAM

**COLLINS
COBUILD**

HarperCollins*Publishers*

Contents

Introduction

The Dictionary

Which of the following pieces of information do you expect to find in a dictionary?

the spelling of a word
the meaning of a word or phrase
the pronunciation of a word, including word stress
the synonyms and antonyms of a word
the collocations (words that often go together)
the usage (how a word is used)
the grammar of a word
the register (formal, informal, spoken, written, etc.)
real examples

The Collins COBUILD English Dictionary gives you all of this information.

When you use the dictionary to look up a word, it is important for you, as a learner, to understand all the information that is given. In this way you will be able to build your active vocabulary, rather than just your passive knowledge.

The dictionary is not just an excellent reference tool; it is also a way of exploring the English language.

The Workbook

This workbook is designed to accompany the Collins COBUILD English Dictionary. Its aim is to familiarize students with the information contained in the dictionary and to show them how to get the best out of it.

All the material in this workbook may be photocopied within an institution and can be used in class or for self-study. An answer key is provided at the back of the book. Each page of exercises is independent of any other page, and both teachers and students should feel free to start wherever they want.

The exercises are aimed at students of an upper-intermediate level, making the workbook suitable for use in the last years of secondary school, at the outset of a university course, or with adult students of Cambridge *First Certificate* level or above.

The workbook is divided into six sections:

1 **Finding Words and Phrases** trains students in basic reference skills and helps them to find their way around the dictionary, showing them where they can find particular entries. It is important that students know where such items as phrasal verbs, phrases, and compound nouns are defined, so that they can find them quickly. This section will give learners confidence in using the dictionary.

2 **Using the Explanations and Examples** shows students how to get a lot of information from the explanations (or definitions) and from the examples. The explanations show, for example, the typical context a word is used in, and also give information about style and usage. By doing these exercises students will realize how much they can learn from the explanations and examples when they know what to look for.

3 **Using the Grammatical Information** shows students both how to find the relevant information about grammar and how to use it when they have found it. In particular, there is practice in using the Extra Column, which is unique to COBUILD dictionaries, giving clear and quick access to the grammar.

4 **Using the Phonetics** deals with pronunciation. This section gives students practice in both reading and writing phonetics, and in word stress, homographs, and homophones.

5 **Looking at Meaning** covers synonyms, antonyms, words with multiple meanings, and pragmatics (how language is actually used and how people interpret what is said or written). The dictionary has a lot of information on pragmatic uses because these are important for learners if they are going to communicate effectively in English.

6 **Looking at Very Common Words** shows learners how to understand and use these entries, which are sometimes long and fairly complicated.

One of the most important aims of the Collins COBUILD English Dictionary is to help students produce for themselves more accurate and more natural language. This workbook shows students how they can get the most out of their dictionary and how sensible use of it can help them produce real English. We hope that by working through the exercises in this workbook students will gain confidence in their own abilities and will, therefore, progress in their knowledge and enjoyment of the language.

Alphabetical Ordering

The Alphabet

Finding words in a dictionary is not always easy.
Even native speakers sometimes fail to find words
that are there.

If your own language is written in Roman script,
you will be used to looking up words in alphabetical
order. If your own language is written in a different
script, you may find it more difficult to look up
words in the Roman alphabet.

Write out the letters of the alphabet as they are
ordered in English. You can consult this table later if
you need to.

1	2	3	4	5	6	7	8	9	10	11	12	13
A												

14	15	16	17	18	19	20	21	22	23	24	25	26

2 Alphabetical Disorder!

This list is even more confusing! Put the words in
the correct alphabetical order.

distinguished	1 _____
distinctive	2 _____
disintegrate	3 _____
disinterested	4 _____
district	5 _____
distribution	6 _____
distributor	7 _____
destruction	8 _____
destructive	9 _____
distortion	10 _____

1 Alphabetical Ordering

As well as looking at the first letter of a word, you
usually need to check the second, third, or later
letters of a word. Here are some lists of words. Each
list is arranged alphabetically - well, not quite!
Which word or words in each list should be moved
and where to?

1	2	3	4	5
apple	anteater	readily	miserable	underestimate
apron	antecedent	readjust	miserly	underdeveloped
bread	antelope	rebate	misery	underfoot
cupboard	anemone	rebellious	mishap	underhand
cupola	antique	redness	missionary	underlie
couple	antonym	redistribute	missing	underling
disagreeable	anvil	reed	misspell	undeveloped
disappointing	anywhere	reference	mistake	undeserved
			mistime	unreserved
			misshapen	unnerve

Compounds

Compound words (such as 'breakfast time' and 'breakfast television') are very common in English, and this dictionary has a lot of useful information about them. These combinations have a main entry when they are thought of as 'compounds' by native speakers. This means that native speakers think of the combination as if it were one word in meaning. Some of these compounds have become one word.

1 Compounds and Alphabetical Ordering

Compounds follow the usual rules for alphabetical ordering. These words all begin with **brea**. Look in the dictionary and put them in alphabetical order:

breadboard	1 _____
breakfast time	2 _____
bread	3 _____
breakdown	4 _____
break-in	5 _____
breakthrough	6 _____
breakfast	7 _____
breadth	8 _____
breakable	9 _____
breakfast television	10 _____

You will have noticed that we ignore spaces and hyphens, and treat these compounds as one word.

2 How to Write Compounds

How are two-word expressions written? There are three possibilities:

Two words	tail end
With a hyphen	tail-light
One word	tailgate

Sometimes there is more than one possibility for a compound. In this case the dictionary gives the most common use first and then tells you about the alternative spelling. Look at this entry for **breakfast time**:

> **breakfast time**; also spelled **breakfast-time.** N-UNCOUNT:
> **Breakfast time** is the period of the morning oft prep N
> when most people have their breakfast. *By breakfast-time he was already at his desk.*

This is a very difficult area of English, and the language is constantly changing. What often happens is that a compound starts as two words, is then hyphenated, and finally ends up as one word.

Imagine that the word **second** is attached to each of the following words. How would you write it?

1 _____	best
2 _____	class
3 _____	cousin
4 _____	hand
5 _____	language
6 _____	opinion
7 _____	rate

Imagine that the word **night** is attached to each of the following words. How would you write it?

8 _____	club
9 _____	gown
10 _____	life
11 _____	mare
12 _____	owl
13 _____	time
14 _____	watchman

Check in the dictionary to see whether you agree with it!

Choose any two pages of the dictionary and see how many compounds you can find.

? Did you know....?
The word which occurs in the most compounds is **SELF.**

Spelling

Looking up a word in the dictionary is easy if you are quite certain how it is spelled. But one important use of the dictionary is to check spellings that you are not certain about. Usually, you know how a word begins, but perhaps not always!

Have you ever confused these two words?

affect/effect

If you look up **affect** under **e**, you obviously will not find it. The pronunciations of these two words are similar, so unless your pronunciation is better than your spelling, you might have trouble!

1 A or E?

Complete the beginnings of the incomplete words in these sentences. When you've finished, check your answers in the dictionary by looking at the examples in both entries.

1 Susan was greatly ____ffected by his death.

2 His death had a terrible ____ffect on her.

3 When does the new law come into ____ffect?

4 More than seven million people have been ____ffected by drought.

5 Arthritis is a crippling disease which ____ffects people all over the world.

6 It's certainly going to ____ffect our budget for next year.

2 Confusing Spellings

Small spelling differences in words which are pronounced the same or almost the same are difficult even for native speakers. Sometimes the words have completely different meanings, but sometimes their meanings are related in some way. Often the difference is also a difference of grammar. For example, the meanings of **practise** and **practice** are related, but **practise** is a verb, and **practice** is a noun. However, the words **stationary** and **stationery** are not related at all in meaning. In this case, **stationary** is an adjective, and **stationery** is a noun.

To the right are pairs of easily confusable words. Each word has one or more letters missing. Complete the words with the missing letters. Under each pair of words are two examples with one of the

two words missing. Choose the correct word from each pair for each example. Then check your answers in the dictionary.

1 l ___ se/l ___ se

  a ...a few _____ sheets of paper.

  b They expected to _____ the election.

2 princip ___ /princip ___

  a His _____ interest in life was to be rich.

  b ...the _____ of acceleration.

3 practi ___ e/practi ___ e

  a Many doctors _____ from their own houses.

  b ...a doctor with a private _____ .

4 station ___ ry/station ___ ry

  a Use the handbrake when your vehicle is _____ .

  b He had a shop which sold _____ .

5 advi ___ e/advi ___ e

  a She went to a psychiatrist for _____ .

  b I would strongly _____ you against buying that car.

6 lic ___ e/lic ___ e

  a The car is _____ d and insured.

  b ...a driving _____ .

7 de ___ ert/de ___ ert

  a ...the Sahara _____ .

  b For _____ there was ice cream.

8 comp ___ ent/comp ___ ent

  a She was a perfect contrast and _____ to Sally.

  b Thanks for the _____ .

Rules for spelling in English are complicated. However, when you cannot find a word and you think that is because you cannot spell it properly, there are a couple of things you can try:

1 Ask yourself if you are pronouncing the word properly.
2 Write down possible alternative spellings, cross out unlikely ones and look up the rest.

Phrases 1

In English there are a lot of expressions which consist of two or more words. Many of these are phrasal verbs, which are dealt with in the next section. Many others are expressions or fixed phrases. The dictionary contains explanations of many of these, but it is sometimes difficult to know where to find them.

How to Find Phrases

Here is part of the dictionary entry for **mouth**:

9 If you **keep** your **mouth shut** about something, you do not talk about it, especially because it is a secret. *You wouldn't be here now if she'd kept her mouth shut.*
10 • **live hand to mouth**: see **hand**. • **heart in** your **mouth**: see **heart**. • **from the horse's mouth**: see **horse**. • to **put** your **money where** your **mouth is**: see **money**. • **shut** your **mouth**: see **shut**. • **born with a silver spoon in** your **mouth**: see **spoon**. • **word of mouth**: see **word**. • **put words into** someone's **mouth**: see **word**.

V and N inflect
= keep quiet

As you can see from the paragraph numbers (9 and 10), phrases come at the end of the entry for **mouth**. You will also see that in paragraph 9, the phrase **keep** your **mouth shut** is explained, but in paragraph 10 the phrases are not explained. You are given an instruction to 'see …'. This means that if you want to know more about the phrase **born with a silver spoon in** your **mouth**, you have to look up the word **spoon**.

Phrases are usually explained at the least common word or at the noun, and this is why **born with a silver spoon in** your **mouth** is explained at **spoon** and not at **mouth**.

Look up the eight phrases in paragraph 10 and write the example sentences (if there are no example sentences, write the definition) for each below:

1 _____

2 _____

3 _____

4 _____

5 _____

6 _____

7 _____

8 _____

❓ *Did you know….?*

The dictionary entry with the most phrases is **WAY**. It has sixty-seven phrases.

Phrases 2

Eye

Look at the entry for **eye.** This is a word which is used in a large number of phrases, some of which are explained at **eye** and others of which are cross-referenced to other words in the dictionary.

The examples in the following table all contain phrases using the word **eye.** First, look at the entry for **eye** to find out where each phrase is explained. Look up each phrase, and then fill in the table, saying where the phrase is explained and giving its paragraph number. Then write the phrase itself. The first one is done for you.

Example	Word at which phrase is explained	Paragraph number	Phrase
1 Just this once, we'll turn a blind eye to what you've done.	blind	11	turn a blind eye
2 Keep an eye on him for me while I'm away, would you?			
3 I've had my eye on her for a long time.			
4 The flowers in the window caught my eye.			
5 John wanted to explain what had happened, but he couldn't catch Mr Craig's eye.			
6 Stop trying to pull the wool over my eyes! What were you two fighting about just now?			
7 In the corner was a little girl crying her eyes out.			
8 Here's something to feast your eyes on - a photo of James.			
9 The Government cannot shut its eyes to the problem of unemployment.			
10 I lost my temper and gave him a black eye.			
11 ...the minister in the eye of the storm.			
12 The planet Mars will be visible to the naked eye all week.			

Phrases 3

1 Where are They?

In the following examples there are some phrases in *italics*. Write down the main entry under which you think you will find the meaning of the phrase. Then check your answers in the dictionary.

1 *The next thing I knew,* _____
   I was in hospital.

2 Fifty pounds will *do nicely* _____
   thank you.

3 I can't see any problems, _____
   but *time will tell.*

4 You won't feel like leaving, _____
   which *is just as well* because
   the government has no
   intention of letting you.

5 *Something like* ninety per _____
   cent of the crop was destroyed.

Now use the phrases in *italics* above to complete these examples.

6 This carpet will _____ in our living

   room.

7 Judging from everything you've said, it

   _____ she wasn't there.

8 Only _____ whether Broughton's

   optimism is justified.

9 I swung round quickly and _____ I

   was looking straight at her.

10 That's the equivalent of _____ two and

   a half per cent a week.

2 View

Look at the dictionary entry for the word **view**. Complete the following sentences, using one of the following phrases:

in my view   in view of

with a view to   in view

on view

1 _____ the fact that she was first, she

   should get the prize.

2 The journalist wrote the story _____

   embarrassing the government.

3 We are, _____, still no further

   forward.

4 In the Van Gogh Museum in Amsterdam, 130 of

   his paintings are _____ .

5 They worked out this whole complicated plot with

   one aim _____ – to gain control of the

   company.

6 The report says that _____ this the UN

   should continue to observe the situation there.

7 _____ the team should have acted

   sooner.

Phrasal Verbs

It is important to realize that phrasal verbs listed in the dictionary are not quite in alphabetical order. They appear together at the end of the entry of the verb from which they are formed and before any other words which come alphabetically after the verb. This is to make it easier for you to find these very common expressions.

1 Phrasal Verbs with Break

Look up the phrasal verbs that start with the verb **break**.

1 How many different _____ meanings of **break away** are given?

2 Which paragraph of **break down** has a machine as the subject of the verb? _____

3 Which paragraphs of **break down** mention a person as the subject of the verb? _____

4 Which paragraph of **break in** has a cross-reference? _____

5 Which phrasal verb in the dictionary comes before the phrasal verb **break up**? _____

6 Which headword in the dictionary comes after the phrasal verb **break up**? _____

2 Phrasal Verbs with Get

How many different phrasal verbs start with the word **get**?

1 How many different particles (that is, adverbs or prepositions) are used after **get**? _____

2 Which combination has the most meanings? _____

3 Match the following sentences to each of the meanings of **get out**. There is one example for each meaning.

Example	Paragraph Number
a We don't get out much together, what with the children being so young.	_____
b If this gets out, we'll lose the contract.	_____
c They can't get out, the army has them surrounded.	_____
d I can't get out of it, I have a contract.	_____

3 Phrasal Verbs with Pull

Make a list of all the phrasal verbs that start with the verb **pull**.

pull away _____   _____

_____   _____

_____   _____

_____   _____

_____   _____

_____   _____

? Did you know....?
The verb with the most phrasal verbs is **GO**.

Someone and Something

In this dictionary, the explanation of a word and the examples that follow it do not only give you information about the meaning of the word; they also often give you information about how the word is typically used.

The exercises in this section show you how to use this information in order to get the best out of your dictionary.

People or Things

Some words are used mainly of people, while others are used mainly of objects or ideas. The explanations and examples tell you whether a word is normally found in one kind of context only.

Look up the word **incapable** and decide which of these sentences it is likely to be used in.

a The car was _____ of being mended.

b She was _____ of stealing.

Each explanation in the dictionary refers to 'someone' who is incapable, and all the examples describe people as incapable. This tells you that we normally use the word to describe people, not machines, which means that (b) is the correct answer.

Now do the same thing with each of the following words (be careful as one of the words can be used with both people and things!) :

1 **unworkable**

   a She turned down all his suggestions as

   _____ without giving them a try.

   b He is _____ in this company.

2 **outmoded**

   a We have an _____ system which has

   existed since the turn of the century.

   b She thought her father was a bit

   _____ .

3 **grandiose**

   a The waiter was _____ in his manner

   towards them.

   b Her _____ schemes have got her into

   debt.

4 **ablaze**

   a Bonfires were already _____ .

   b She was _____ , her skin burning.

5 **rubbish**

   a He described her book as absolute

   _____ .

   b I tried playing golf, but I was _____ .

6 **insensitive**

   a This software is _____ to our needs.

   b I feel my husband is very _____

   about my problem.

7 **cancerous**

   a The energy of the radiation will kill the

   _____ cells.

   b … a hospital which specializes in the treatment

   of _____ patients.

8 **chilling**

   a He was ruthless, _____ , and

   aggressive.

   b The book gives a _____ account of

   the last days of the minister's life.

Word Order

Some words or expressions are used in one position in a sentence more frequently than in any other position. It is not necessarily wrong to use them in another position but it may sound slightly strange or unnatural.

1 The Position of Adverbs

Look up the word **increasingly** and then decide which position in the sentence it would most naturally fill. Choose from those places marked with an asterisk:

I * am * getting * unhappy * about the way things are developing.

The examples talk of things being increasingly difficult, increasingly popular, and so on. This tells you that **increasingly** is typically used immediately before an adjective or verb. The answer is therefore:

…getting **increasingly** unhappy… .

Now do the same thing with each of the following words:

1 **gratefully**	She * took * their charity *.
2 **incomparably**	We * are * better off * than we were a year ago.
3 **particularly**	They don't go out much, * during the winter months *.
4 **incredibly**	The film * was * boring *.

2 The Order of Adjectives

When there is more than one adjective in front of a noun, this is the order you should put them in:

He showed me two very *large white wooden* boxes.

Large is a graded adjective. A graded adjective can be used with an adverb or phrase indicating degree, such as *less, more, very,* etc. Many graded adjectives have comparative and superlative forms.
In the dictionary this information is given in the Extra Column like this:　　　ADJ-GRADED

White is noted in the Extra Column as:　　　COLOUR

Wooden is an ungraded adjective and is noted in the Extra Column as:　　　ADJ
Ungraded adjectives are never or very rarely used with an adverb or phrase indicating degree, e.g. *He has been <u>absent</u> from his desk for two weeks.*

Now put the adjectives given in the correct order in these sentences.

1 **French, small**

Her family ran a _____ _____

restaurant in the theatrical district of the city.

2 **green, small**

His _____ _____ eyes were

surrounded by many wrinkles.

3 **French, wistful**

I sang her a _____ _____ ballad.

4 **soft, yellow**

The small lamp on the table made a

_____ _____ glow all around her.

5 **huge, gilt**

_____ _____ earrings dangled

from her ears.

6 **woollen, white**

The baby was tightly wrapped in a

_____ _____ shawl.

7 **Chinese, young**

Karen had made friends with some

_____ _____ girls.

8 **long, unbroken**

In the _____ _____ silence which

followed she realized that he had fallen asleep.

9 **check, old, pink**

A potted plant stood on the

_____ _____ _____ cloth.

Verbs

1 Verbs and their Subjects

Apart from the meaning, a great deal of other information is given in the explanation of the words. Look at the way verbs are explained in the dictionary:

A If the verb refers to something that most people might do, the explanation usually begins 'If you ... '. For example, 'If you **ask** someone something, you say something to them in the form of a question ... '.

B If the verb refers to something that not very many people do or that we think people should not be encouraged to do, the explanation usually begins 'If someone ... '. For example, 'If someone or something **bores** you, you find them dull and uninteresting'.

C If the subject of the verb is usually not a person but a thing, the explanation begins 'If something ... '. For example, 'If something **adheres** to something else, it sticks firmly to it'.

You will also find other ways of beginning the explanations of verbs in the dictionary. When you do, try to think why the particular words that have been chosen have been used.

Which of the three forms of words that have been explained in the left-hand column do you think are used in the dictionary for the verbs in the following sentences?

Examples	A, B, or C?
1 He *kicked* the ball over the hedge.	_____
2 She wanted to *borrow* my book.	_____
3 Some of the crowd *attempted* to break through.	_____
4 They started to *swear* and shout.	_____
5 He *nodded* his head.	_____
6 The strange sight surprised and *alarmed* me.	_____
7 These drugs *inhibit* the animals' development.	_____
8 I watched bombs *obliterate* the villages.	_____

2 When or If?

Now look at another feature of the way verbs are explained in the dictionary:

A If the verb refers to something that someone regularly or typically does, the explanation usually begins 'When you ... '. For example, 'When you **cough**, you force air out of your throat with a sudden, harsh noise ... '.

B If the verb refers to something that someone does only occasionally, or that not everyone does, the explanation usually begins 'If you ... '. For example, 'If you **resign** from a job or position, you formally announce that you are leaving it.'

Which of the two forms of words that have been used in the left-hand column do you think are used in the dictionary in the following sentences?

Examples	A or B?
1 Relax your muscles and *breathe* deeply.	_____
2 He *died* in 1987, aged seventy.	_____
3 Then she *broke down* in tears.	_____
4 One day a larger ship *anchored* offshore.	_____
5 The authorities had taken the decision to *deport* him.	_____

Collocations 1

Collocations are words that go together. It is not always enough to know the meaning of a word for you to be able to use it appropriately. You have to know the collocates of the word: the words that most frequently occur with it. The dictionary gives a lot of information on collocations. Look at these two paragraphs from **fast**:

> 6 If you hold **fast** to a principle or idea, or if you stand **fast**, you do not change your mind about it, even though people are trying to persuade you to. *We can only try to hold fast to the age-old values of honesty, decency and concern for others... He told reporters to stand fast over the next few vital days.*

This tells you the two verbs (**hold** and **stand**) that are usually used with this meaning of **fast**.

> 10 Someone who is **fast asleep** is completely asleep. *When he went upstairs five minutes later, she was fast asleep.*

Here the collocation is a phrase and is therefore in bold: **fast asleep**.

1 Adjectives

Many adjectives in English are used with only a small selection of nouns. Using the information in the explanations and examples, say what sorts of words these adjectives are used with. The first one has been done for you.

Adjective used with

1 scorching	weather, temperatures, day
2 daunting	_____
3 biting (paragraph 1)	_____
4 purpose-built	_____
5 auburn	_____
6 chequered (paragraph 1)	_____
7 acrid	_____
8 back-breaking	_____

2 Adverbs and Adjectives

Some adverbs and adjectives are very commonly used with only one other word. You will often find that they are used in this way simply to give emphasis to the word that follows. For example, 'if someone is **dead tired**, they are very tired indeed.' Sometimes these collocations are shown as phrases in the dictionary, and sometimes they are shown in the explanations.

Use the dictionary to help you fill in the missing words below.

1 I've been awake since dawn. Chris is still sound

_____ in the other bed.

2 There was a sudden outbreak of thunder and

lightning with torrential _____ .

3 Other inventions, such as the Bell picturephone,

have hardly been a roaring _____ .

4 They were filthy _____ . They had a

huge house in London and another in the south of

France.

5 Now I've got my own house I'm always flat

_____ .

6 ... the completion of a spanking _____

motorway linking Rio de Janeiro to the city centre.

7 They ate in restaurants ranging from the vastly

expensive to the dirt-_____ .

Collocations 2

1 Common Verbs and Nouns

Many common verbs like **do, have, make, set,** and **take** form collocations with certain nouns. In these collocations, most of the meaning is carried by the nouns they are associated with.

Underline the verb + noun collocations in these examples.

1 He would never have thought of making a telephone call to the police to tell them where it was.

2 There may be other ways to persuade students to do homework without making it compulsory.

3 Sorry, we made a mistake. Your blood test got mixed up with someone else's.

4 Do you think that the Royal Family should set an example when it comes to marriage?

5 Tomorrow afternoon we'll return the library books and do some shopping!

Now, using the verb + noun combinations you found above, complete the examples below.

6 The White House Budget Office cut its staff nearly

in half to _____ for other agencies.

7 Mrs Howard had driven in with her to

_____ .

8 Yesterday, he _____ to his wife

Gabrielle in Paris.

9 He had _____ his _____

quite thoroughly before he arrived in

Johannesburg.

10 He was scared to admit he'd _____ .

2 Do or Make?

Complete these jokes and quotations with the correct form of **do** or **make**.

1 I hate housework. You _____ the beds,

you _____ the dishes. And six months

later you have to start all over again.

Joan Rivers

2 If I wasn't _____ mistakes, I wasn't

_____ decisions.

Robert W. Johnson

3 Wife: Cooking! Cleaning! Why should women

_____ it?

Husband: You're right. Let's get an au pair girl.

4 I don't _____ jokes, I just watch the

government and report the facts.

Will Rogers

3 Give or Hold?

Complete these newspaper headlines with the correct form of **give** or **hold**.

1 Brazil's new president _____ first speech.

2 South African government to _____ emergency meeting.

3 Mia Farrow _____ star performance in court.

4 Somalia's factions _____ peace talks.

Style and Usage 1

1 Style and Register

A lot of words and expressions in English can be used in one kind of situation, but not in others. For example, in a letter to a friend, you might say that you went to a **grotty** restaurant, but if you are writing a letter of complaint, in formal English, you would not describe something as **grotty**, because **grotty** is a very informal word meaning 'awful'.

Many words are found in particular kinds of English, such as formal, informal, technical, literary, or old-fashioned language, or only in American or British English. The dictionary gives you this information, in addition to telling you about meaning. Words which are suitable for use in most contexts are not identified in this way.

Look up the following words in the dictionary and find out what the dictionary says about the way that they are used. Write the information you find in the space provided.

Words	Style and Register
1 aubergine	_____
2 bookstore	_____
3 whoops	_____
4 frock	_____
5 belated	_____
6 breach of the peace	_____
7 anterior	_____
8 get stuffed (get 3)	_____
9 decaf	_____
10 car-jacker	_____
11 amortize	_____
12 bespectacled	_____
13 besmirch	_____

2 Informal or Formal?

Look at the words in *italics* in these pairs of examples and say which ones you think are **informal**. When you've finished, look them up in the dictionary to check your answers.

1 a When I was a *child* I lived in a country village.

  b All the *kids* in my class could read.

2 a He's living with his mum and *dad*.

  b He would be a good *father* to my children.

3 a She turned the *television* on and flicked around between news programmes.

  b After a hard day's work most people want to relax in front of the *telly*.

4 a Beer cost three *pounds* a bottle.

  b It cost him five hundred *quid*.

Style and Usage 2

American or British?

Look at the following examples and say whether the word in *italics* is British English or American English. Then write the equivalent word in the other language in the space provided. Use your dictionary to help you.

Examples	British or American	Equivalent?
1 This requires having an extra *tap* in the kitchen.		
2 He raised the *hood* of McKee's truck.		
3 The park was full of people – kids playing, mothers pushing babies in *strollers*.		
4 Take your valuables with you or lock them in the *boot*.		
5 Suddenly, he was terrified of the *motorway*.		
6 Charles walked slowly down the *sidewalk*.		
7 He slipped into corduroy *trousers* and a white shirt.		
8 He had almost half a tank of *gasoline*.		
9 I took the *elevator* to the twenty-first floor.		
10 Leonard first heard it while he was waiting in the *queue*.		
11 Under her chest of drawers was a rather stale chocolate *biscuit*.		
12 An odor of rotting fruit rose from the *garbage* bin next to the sink.		

Look at the following examples of British English and say why the words in *italics* may cause problems for someone who speaks American English. Check the words in your dictionary.

	British meaning	American meaning
13 He asked me to take him indoors and help him *wash up*.		
14 He is to *table* questions to the Prime Minister today.		
15 He sleeps on the *first floor*.		
16 It costs twice as much to educate a pupil at a *public school* as at a state equivalent.		

Parts of Speech

The COBUILD *dictionary* does not *just give* you *information about*
the *meaning of words*, it *also gives* you *useful information about* their *grammar*.
This *information is shown clearly* and *concisely in* the Extra Column.

1 What Part of Speech is it?

Look back at the words in *italics* in the two sentences above and find examples of these parts of speech:

1 Nouns   _____

2 Verbs   _____

3 Adjectives   _____

4 Adverbs   _____

5 Prepositions   _____

2 Nouns, Verbs, Adjectives, Adverbs, and Prepositions

Look up these words in the dictionary: **down, house, right, round, good, ring, well, work.**
Each of these words belongs to more than one word class.
Write the correct word in the sentences below and show the word class:

1 a As I drove _____ that mountain, day was ending.   _____

  b They managed to _____ two bottles of wine.   _____

  c He put the tray _____ on the table at her side.   _____

2 a What am I going to do with these diamond _____ ?   _____

  b The phone _____ about 200 times a day.   _____

3 a What sort of _____ are you thinking of doing?   _____

  b The system allows people to _____ together.   _____

4 a The building now _____ 150 monks.   _____

  b The number of new _____ being built is rising fast.   _____

5 a He's very _____ at telling people what they want to hear. _____

  b She is too smart for her own _____ .   _____

6 a It proved that they had made the _____ decision.   _____

  b A main highway runs _____ through the area.   _____

  c He managed to _____ the boat and get in it.   _____

7 a Sue got a sympathetic _____ of applause.   _____

  b She had small feet and hands and a flat _____ face.   _____

  c They needed some way of getting _____ the country.   _____

  d ... a murderer waiting for his victim to _____ the corner. _____

8 a Resentful workers will not do anything _____ .   _____

  b Women gathered water from the _____ , shopped, and marketed. _____

Verbs 1

1 Verb Patterns

Here is a list of some of the main verb patterns, followed by some sentences. After each sentence, put in the appropriate verb pattern.

Example:

Her boyfriend *gave* her a diamond ring.   <u>**V n n**</u>

Patterns:

V	V prep/adv	V with quote
V that	V n	V pron-refl
V to-inf	V -ing	V n n
V n *into* -ing	V n to-inf	V n adj

Sentences

1 I *can't bear* to think of time passing.   _____

2 The police are refusing to *call* it an assassination.   _____

3 Please *cancel* my appointments for the rest of the day.   _____

4 He *glanced* at his watch.   _____

5 'I disapprove of hunting, myself,' she *said*.   _____

6 *Enjoy* yourself more.   _____

7 The accused refuses to *admit* that it was wrong to use force.   _____

8 The jury *found* her guilty of second-degree murder.   _____

9 One evening he *asked* me to go out and have a cup of coffee with him.   _____

10 Henry *charmed* people into parting with thousands of pounds.   _____

11 My lawyer called the bank to find out what *had occurred*.   _____

12 She *regretted* having revealed so much of her life to him.   _____

2 Verbs Followed by Prepositional Phrases

Some verbs have the pattern **V prep**, or a pattern with a specified preposition such as **V in n**. Complete the following sentences with the correct preposition from the list below. When you've finished, look up the verbs in the dictionary to check your answers.

on   about   to   in   for   from

1 They *were arguing* _____ politics as they played.

2 The house *had belonged* _____ her family for three generations.

3 Mr Hattersley *concentrated* particularly _____ the provisions made for women in the social charter.

4 After leaving university, Therese *decided* _____ a career in publishing.

5 The cooking time *depends* _____ the size of the potato.

6 I used to sit and *worry* _____ my future.

7 Money can't buy happiness, but it helps you *look* _____ it in a lot more places.

8 A lawyer is someone who *prevents* someone else _____ getting your money.

9 They *objected* _____ the cigarette smoke with which he filled the room.

10 They *rely* _____ firewood for cooking.

11 All countries are expected to *succeed* _____ bringing down inflation this year.

Verbs 2

Most verbs are just labelled **VERB**; they have no class. Two exceptions are **V-ERG** and **V-RECIP**.

1 V-ERG: ergative verb

Read the description of ergative verbs in the Introduction to the dictionary.
You will see that ergative verbs usually have the patterns **V** or **V prep/adv**, and **V n** or **V n prep/adv**.
Look at these sentences and give each one the correct pattern.

1 a The bomb did not *explode* and no-one was hurt.   _____

  b The message contained a threat to *explode* a bomb in New York City.   _____

2 a Wade pulled out his keys and *opened* the door.   _____

  b The door *opened* quietly and Marie came in.   _____

3 a I *bounced* a ball against the house.   _____

  b A big red rubber ball *bounced* suddenly across his field of vision.   _____

4 a He waited for the water to *boil*.   _____

  b *Boil* drinking water for at least ten minutes.   _____

5 a Be conscious of social injustices but do not try to *change* the world at one go.   _____

  b The ten-year-olds in class five have seen the world *change* around them.   _____

6 a The bottle *smashed* against a wall.   _____

  b He was attacked in a disco by a man who *smashed* a beer glass into his face.   _____

2 V-RECIP: reciprocal verb

Read the description of reciprocal verbs in the Introduction to the dictionary. There are different types of
reciprocal verb: one type usually has the patterns **pl-n V** and **V with n**; another type has the patterns **pl-n V**
and **V n**; and a third has the patterns **pl-n V n** and **V n with n**. Look at these sentences and give each one the
correct pattern.

1 a She failed her O-level exams and *argued* with her teachers.   _____

  b The children are always *arguing*. They really hate each other.   _____

2 a My mother *has* never *communicated* with me.   _____

  b We *are communicating* like a manager and player should.   _____

3 a The lawyer said that his client intended to *cooperate* with the subcommittee.   _____

  b The two countries agreed to *cooperate* in addressing air-pollution problems.   _____

4 a I can't bear to think of people *gossiping* behind my back.   _____

  b I ought to be getting on with my work instead of *gossiping* with him.   _____

5 a She clung to the memory of her vanished husband and refused to *divorce* him.   _____

  b We have split up, but we *have* never *divorced*.   _____

6 a Italy *negotiated* a treaty of cooperation with the United States.   _____

  b Britain and Vietnam say they *have negotiated* a new deal.   _____

Nouns 1

1 Count, Uncount, and Variable Nouns

Look in the Introduction to the dictionary for explanations of **N-COUNT**, **N-UNCOUNT**, and **N-VAR**.
Then look at each of the sets of sentences below and say which class the noun in *italics* belongs to.
Check your answers in the dictionary.

1 No one had lived in the house for decades, but it was still full of *furniture*.
  The *furniture* is a mixture of old and new.
  Every single piece of *furniture* is original.   _____

2 He was standing in a vast hall lined with gilded *mirrors*.
  It was like looking in a *mirror*.
  Moira glanced at Liz's reflection in her *mirror*.   _____

3 There was abundant vegetation to satisfy the *appetites* of the plant-eating dinosaurs.
  They ate without *appetite*, almost in silence.
  He has a healthy *appetite*.   _____

4 If today's talks lead to negotiations, a *compromise* is the most likely outcome.
  He is a cautious man who favours *compromise*.
  Have you had to make *compromises*?   _____

5 All I can do is assemble *information* that I've received.
  For an informed choice, lots of *information* is needed.
  Shouldn't I take this *information* to them?   _____

6 Healthy *bones* are among the benefits that can result from a balanced diet.
  One of the functions of *bone* is to store calcium.
  The cricketer broke a *bone* in his left hand.   _____

7 Do you feel the need for an *aim* in life?
  One of the *aims* of the study was to measure the effects of radiation.
  What was his main *aim* when he was setting it up?   _____

2 Nouns with Different Behaviour Patterns

Some nouns sometimes have different patterns from the normal behaviour for that word class.
This behaviour is shown in the dictionary with 'also'. Look up the words **agony, lack,** and **paperback**
in the dictionary and fit the words into the following sentences:

1 Too little eye contact might be regarded as a sign of dishonesty or _____ of interest.

  A _____ of medicine was the reason for the deaths, he said.

2 When I tried to move, a stab of _____ shot up my thigh.

  Eczema is not usually life-threatening but its _____ are like the slow drip-drip of a tap.

3 On the table sits a _____ of his new autobiography.

  The book first began to make his reputation after it was published in _____ in 1986.

Nouns 2

1 Noun Patterns 1

Here are some of the noun patterns that you will see in the dictionary.
In each case, capital **N** stands for the noun **in the entry**.

N *of* n	poss N	N *to* n	adj N	*in* N
N n	n N	N *for* n	N to-inf	N that

Look at these sentences and give each one the correct pattern.
In each sentence, the noun in the entry is in *italics*.

1 The government honoured a *promise* to hold elections in 1990.   _____

2 She remembered her *childhood* as one long, sunny idyll.   _____

3 She had always been a smart *dresser*.   _____

4 We marched on to the *hilltop* village of Monteriggioni.   _____

5 There has never been any *suggestion* that his action is other than right.   _____

6 This month Hipwood takes over as *captain* of the England team.   _____

7 There was plenty of *opportunity* for discussion after the meeting.   _____

8 We looked at each other in *amazement*.   _____

9 He saved up to start his own business, including a clothing *factory*.   _____

10 He was declared a *traitor* to the Crown.   _____

2 Noun Patterns 2

Look in the Introduction to the dictionary for explanations of **supp** and **poss** and their patterns.
Then look at these sentences and underline the words which are part of the pattern.

1 **N with supp**
   a She has made her first *appearance* before a special court in Basingstoke.
   b It folds away for easy storage - an *aspect* which most parents will find appealing.
   c Underneath is a *diagram* showing how the views of the two eyes overlap.
   d Repeat the movement two or three times in the same *direction*.

2 **supp N**
   a Should America be giving humanitarian *aid*?
   b It had to be a man who knew the theatre *crowd*.
   c My 1947 *edition* of the dictionary describes the wellington as being worn by women and children.

3 **N with poss**
   a He had recovered from his flight and the shock of his *arrival*.
   b Detroit was an ideal spot for the *birth* of the mass-produced automobile.
   c The triads are Hong Kong's *equivalent* of the Mafia.

Adjectives 1

1 Graded and Ungraded Adjectives

Adjectives which are sometimes modified with a grading word such as *fairly, more, so,* or *very* (graded adjectives) are labelled **ADJ-GRADED** in the dictionary. Adjectives which are rarely or never modified in that way (ungraded adjectives) are labelled **ADJ**. Often, an adjective has one sense in which it is a graded adjective and one sense in which it is an ungraded adjective. Look up the adjectives in the sentences below and say whether the adjective is graded or ungraded.

1 a Most of the staff were *outgoing*, energetic, and enthusiastic.   _____

  b In the *outgoing* national assembly, the National Front held 25 seats.   _____

2 a The championships were run by the *athletic* club.   _____

  b Barry was a pleasant, *athletic* sort of a guy from New York.   _____

3 a He proved himself to be a more *cold-blooded* businessman than his father.   _____

  b Some *cold-blooded* fish can swim in sub-zero temperatures.   _____

4 a You can get more *emotional* satisfaction from exercise by adding music.   _____

  b Mr Mandela was given an *emotional* welcome from the ruler of Transkei.   _____

Now rewrite the sentences which have graded adjectives but no grading word
so that they contain a grading word:

outgoing _____

athletic _____

emotional _____

2 Positions of Adjectives

In the dictionary, adjectives which always or usually come before nouns are labelled **ADJ n**, and adjectives which always or usually come after link verbs are labelled **v-link ADJ**. Adjectives which do not have either of these labels are used in both positions. Look up the adjectives in these sentences and show whether they are **ADJ n**, **v-link ADJ**, or **both**.

1 When I was a child I was *happy*.   _____

2 What Beth has said is *absolute* nonsense.   _____

3 At the end of 1986, Mr Gates took over as *acting* director.   _____

4 If you follow these simple guidelines you'll feel *better*.   _____

5 Are you a *tidy* person?   _____

6 What do you mean I've got money? I'm as *broke* as you are.   _____

Adjectives 2

1 Adjective Patterns 1

Here is a list of some of the main adjective patterns, followed by some sentences.
After each sentence, put in the appropriate adjective pattern.
Remember that **that** clauses do not always begin with the word *that*.
When you've finished, look up the adjectives in the dictionary to check your answers.

Patterns: ADJ *to* n   ADJ that
            ADJ *of* n   ADJ *about* n
            ADJ to-inf   *it* v-link ADJ to-inf

1 He was as *blind* to her feelings as she was to his.   _____

2 Doctors have remained *cautious* about the results of the treatment.   _____

3 'We were *glad* you could come,' said Leonard.   _____

4 They all greeted me very cordially and were *eager* to talk about the project.   _____

5 They are keenly *aware* of the desperate needs of their people.   _____

6 It is *difficult* to write and express gratitude to a person you don't know.   _____

7 He would not have recognized her, of that he felt *certain*.   _____

8 He was *disgusted* and bitterly *disappointed* that he had lost the cargo.   _____

2 Adjective Patterns 2

Here are some sentences which have been split apart and jumbled up.
Draw arrows between the right and left hand parts to indicate which parts belong together.
If you need to, look up the adjective in the dictionary, find the appropriate sense, and find
out which patterns it has.

1 They are cautiously *optimistic*   a to be insulted in the street.
2 He was thought to be *fit*   b with her husband's sales methods.
3 It cannot have been very *pleasant*   c that the improvement will be maintained.
4 She became *familiar*   d to this kind of project.
5 We are particularly *fond*   e in fruit and vegetables.
6 I am very *sympathetic*   f on a guarantee of safety.
7 He made his departure *conditional*   g of listening to music.
8 His diet is *deficient*   h to play at the weekend.

? *Did you know....?*

You can use the pattern **it v-link ADJ that** to introduce a comment that you want to make.

... it is clear that ...   ... it is important that ...

... it is vital that ...

... it is impossible that ...   ... it is said that ...

Adverbs

1 Adverb Patterns

Here is a list of some of the main adverb patterns.

ADV with v
ADV adj/adv
ADV with cl
ADV -ed

Match these patterns with the examples below. The adverb is in *italics* in each example.
When you've finished, look up the adverbs in the dictionary to check your answers.

1 Since the mid-1950s, *however*, all member governments have expressed support for more
attention to this critical area.
It was a brilliant film. *However*, the movie did have its critics.
There are two kinds of maturity, *however*. There is that of a traditional society, where...

Pattern _____

2 The commission *quickly* concluded that there was a need to strengthen the English and
mathematics courses.
The known facts are few and can be summarized *quickly*.

Pattern _____

3 You know *perfectly* well what happened.
Can you imagine someone throwing a *perfectly* good book in the middle of the street?

Pattern _____

4 During the first week, the evening meetings were *poorly* attended...

Pattern _____

2 Just

Here is a list of the most common adverbial patterns
of **just**.

ADV before v
ADV *about/going* to-inf
ADV adv/prep
ADV n

Match these patterns with the examples on the
right. When you've finished, look up the first five
adverb uses of **just** in the dictionary to check your
answers.

1 Randall would just now be getting the Sunday
paper.

Pattern _____

2 The Vietnam War was just about to end.

Pattern _____

3 That's just one example of the kind of experiments
you can do.

Pattern _____

4 I've just bought a new house.

Pattern _____

Consonants and Short Vowels

The spelling of English words is not always a good guide to how they are pronounced.
For this reason, the dictionary shows you how to pronounce each word using the symbols of the International Phonetic Alphabet (IPA). A key to these symbols is given on page xxxviii of the dictionary.

1 Consonants

There are 25 consonant symbols. Most of the consonant symbols are written the same as the normal letters e.g. bed is written in phonetics like this: /bed/. There are only eight consonants which have special symbols. These are:

/ ʃ ʒ ŋ tʃ θ ð dʒ j /

Match these special symbols with the words to the right. The sounds you are looking for are underlined and in **bold**.

Word	Symbol	Word	Symbol
1 mea<u>s</u>ure	_____	5 **sh**ip	_____
2 **j**oy	_____	6 **th**in	_____
3 **y**ellow	_____	7 **th**en	_____
4 **ch**eap	_____	8 si**ng**	_____

The most difficult symbols are the vowel symbols and there are 22 of them! Here we have divided them into three sections: short vowels, long vowels, and combinations of vowel sounds.

2 Short Vowels   / æ e ɪ ɒ ʊ ʌ ə i u /

Each sentence below has at least three examples of one of the sounds above.
Use your dictionary to match the sounds with the sentences.

	Symbol	How many?
1 Fit children find a winning system.	_____	_____
2 They could put the wood in the shed.	_____	_____
3 My friend said he went to bed wet.	_____	_____
4 The bad man sat on a mat.	_____	_____
5 Blood! I've cut myself! I must get some help.	_____	_____
6 The teacher is in danger.	_____	_____
7 I spotted a lot of lost dogs.	_____	_____
8 … factual errors about the actual number of casualties.	_____	_____
9 We created very many jobs	_____	_____

Choose a word, which will be easy for you to remember, from each sentence above and write it next to the phonetic symbol.

æ _____	e _____	ɪ _____	ɒ _____
ʊ _____	ʌ _____	ə _____	i _____
u _____			

Long Vowels and Vowel Combinations

1 Long Vowels   / ɑː iː ɔː uː ɜː /

Each sentence below has at least three examples of one of the sounds above.
Use your dictionary to match the sounds with the sentences.

	Symbol	How many?
1 We beat the team.	_____	_____
2 More than four balls were caught.	_____	_____
3 At last my heart started to calm down.	_____	_____
4 The first bird earned the third worm.	_____	_____
5 You choose if we use the shoe or the boot.	_____	_____

Choose a word, which will be easy for you to remember, from each sentence above and write it next to the phonetic symbol.

ɑː _____   iː _____   ɔː _____

uː _____   ɜː _____

2 Vowel Combinations   / aɪ aɪə aʊ aʊə eɪ eə ɪə oʊ ɔɪ ʊə /

Each sentence below has at least two examples of one of the sounds above.
Use your dictionary to match the sounds with the sentences.

	Symbol	How many?
1 I'm sure a cure will help the poor.	_____	_____
2 After a fire it's difficult to find a buyer.	_____	_____
3 It's too loud. Turn it down now or get out!	_____	_____
4 A tower is a sign of power.	_____	_____
5 There must be a place we can get a beer near here.	_____	_____
6 Take care what you wear if you have fair hair.	_____	_____
7 They say a steak makes you put on weight.	_____	_____
8 Give me your coat. There's a note by the phone for you.	_____	_____
9 The lawyer poisoned the boy.	_____	_____
10 I don't mind if you try, but why not buy a guide?	_____	_____

Choose a word, which will be easy for you to remember, from each sentence above
and write it next to the phonetic symbol.

aɪ _____   aɪə _____   aʊ _____   aʊə _____   eɪ _____

eə _____   ɪə _____   oʊ _____   ɔɪ _____   ʊə _____

General Phonetic Practice

1 General Phonetic Practice

Use the key which you have created above or the key on page xxxviii of the dictionary, to work out the spelling of the following words. The first one has been done for you.

Pronunciation	Word		Pronunciation	Word
1 /əbændən/	abandon		11 /ɪnəsənt/	
2 /ɔːgəst/			12 /lʌkʃəri/	
3 /bɪlɒŋ/			13 /meɪbi/	
4 /baʊnd/			14 /ɒbstəkᵊl/	
5 /kæʒuəl/			15 /aʊtsaɪd/	
6 /kraʊd/			16 /oʊzoʊn/	
7 /diːp/			17 /peɪs/	
8 /fɪərs/			18 /peər/	
9 /dʒentᵊl/			19 /rɔː/	
10 /haɪd/			20 /rɪsk/	

2 Vowel Practice

Say these groups of words aloud. Which word in each group has a different vowel sound from the others? Check in the dictionary, if you're not sure.

1 board	2 fur	3 bear	4 put	5 round	6 sail
coat	beard	beer	bus	rough	male
caught	bird	hair	foot	allow	safe
bought	herd	care	good	towel	water

3 American Pronunciation

When American pronunciation differs from the usual British pronunciation, a separate transcription is given of the part of the word that is pronounced differently in American English.

Study this list of words and their phonetic transcriptions. Say each word both ways and decide which pronunciation is which. Write GB by the British pronunciation and AM by the American pronunciation.

1 advertisement	/ædvəˈtaɪzmənt/	_____	/ædvɜːˈtɪsmənt/	_____	/
2 missile	/mɪsaɪl/	_____	/mɪsᵊl/	_____	/
3 thorough	/θɜːroʊ/	_____	/θʌrə/	_____	/
4 tomato	/təmɑːtoʊ/	_____	/təmeɪtoʊ/	_____	/
5 duty	/duːti/	_____	/djuːti/	_____	/

British speakers also pronounce words in different ways. These alternative British pronunciations are also given in the dictionary.

Word Stress

English word stress is very difficult to predict. In fact there are rules, but they are so complicated that it is probably best to learn the stress pattern of a word when you learn the word itself. In the dictionary, stress is shown by <u>underlining</u> the vowel in the stressed syllable.

1 Stress

Say the following words aloud and <u>underline</u> the vowel sound in the stressed syllable. Then check in the dictionary.

1 about   2 area   3 arrive   4 banana   5 camera

6 chocolate   7 enter   8 perhaps   9 potato

10 receive

2 Stress and Compound Words

Compound words also have the stress marked by underlining the vowel sound in the stressed syllable of one of the two words.

Say each of these compound words aloud and <u>underline</u> the stressed vowel sounds. Then check in the dictionary.

1 assembly line   2 heavy metal   3 name-drop

4 bad-tempered   5 high street   6 money-maker

3 Stress and Parts of Speech

Some words in English have the same spelling, but their pronunciation changes depending on what part of speech they are. This pronunciation change is one of stress. Look at this example from the dictionary:

contest, contests, contesting, contested.

The noun is pronounced   /kɒntest/.
The verb is pronounced   /kəntest/.

Read the following pairs of sentences aloud and then <u>underline</u> the stressed sound in the words in *italics*.

1 a The *present* chairperson is a woman.

 b Today I want to *present* the student view.

2 a Keep a *record* of any repair bills.

 b I'd just like to *record* my reservations about the decision.

3 a He is perfectly *content* to remain living in Sweden.

 b The *content* is irrelevant.

4 a It has to have a building *permit*.

 b His poor health wouldn't *permit* it.

5 a The *object* of war is a more perfect peace.

 b Would they *object* to you being an architect?

Now check your answers in the dictionary by looking up each word.

4 Unstressed Syllables

Unstressed syllables are not pronounced very clearly and this is why many non-native speakers of English complain about English people 'eating their words'. These unstressed syllables are an important characteristic of English. Many unstressed syllables contain the vowel /ə/. The vowels /ɪ/ and /ʊ/ are also common in unstressed syllables and when these vowels can be pronounced in different ways, they are transcribed in *italic* script. They are called 'unprotected' vowels.

Say these words aloud and circle the vowel in the unstressed syllable. Then check in the dictionary.

1 photograph   2 doctor   3 different   4 report

5 paper   6 secret   7 release   8 better

Pronunciation, Spelling, and Meaning 1

1 Different Pronunciation, Different Meaning, Same Spelling

Some words in English have the same spelling, but two different meanings and two different pronunciations. Read the following pairs of sentences aloud. Then write a phonetic transcription for each of the words in *italics*. Use the dictionary if you are unsure of the phonetic characters.

Example Sentences   **Phonetic Transcription of the Word**

1 a There was a fierce *wind* blowing.   _____

  b *Wind* the wire round the screws.   _____

2 a He opened the door with a *bow*.   _____

  b Tie it in a *bow*.   _____

3 a The steps *lead* down to his basement.   _____

  b A *lead*-lined bag will protect your films.   _____

4 a … the gentleman in the second *row*.   _____

  b We had a terrible *row* last night.   _____

2 Different Spelling, Different Meaning, Same Pronunciation

Look at the black border in the following advertisement. You will find lots of misspelled words. Read the words aloud. Can you recognize the words now? Rewrite the poem which is in the black border with the correct spelling of all the words. There are sixteen mistakes to find!

_____

_____

_____

_____

_____

_____

_____

_____

Pronunciation, Spelling, and Meaning 2

1 Similar Pronunciation, Different Meaning, Different Spelling

Some words in English have a similar pronunciation to other words, but a different spelling and a different meaning. These words are often used in jokes, especially children's jokes. Read these jokes and see if you can think of another word which has a similar pronunciation to the word in *italics*. Write this word in the space provided· and then check the pronunciation of both words in the dictionary.

1 What's an astronaut's favourite meal?
   Launch.

_____

2 Which country has a good appetite?
   Hungary.

_____

3 Which country has no fat people?
   Finland.

_____

4 What would Switzerland be without all its mountains?
   Alpless.

_____

5 Did you hear about the bike that went round and round biting people?
   It was known as the vicious *cycle.*

_____

6 Where do you weigh whales?
   At the *whale weigh* station.

_____

2 Same Pronunciation, Different Meaning, Different Spelling

These jokes are based on words which have the same pronunciation but a different spelling and meaning (homophones). Read these jokes and see if you can think of another word which has the same pronunciation as the word in italics.
Write this word in the space provided.

1 Have you heard about the author who made a fortune because she was in the *write* business?

_____

2 What did the bell say when it fell in the water?
   I'm *wringing* wet.

_____

3 What do seven days of dieting do?
   They make one *weak.*

_____

4 Estate Agent: This next house hasn't got a *flaw.*
   Customer: What do you walk on then?

_____

5 What's the best way to hunt *bear?*
   With no clothes on.

_____

6 When is a shop like a boat?
   When it has *sales.*

_____

7 What vegetable needs a plumber?
   A *leek.*

_____

8 When is a yellow book not a yellow book?
   When it is *read.*

_____

Synonyms

1 Synonyms

A synonym is a word which means the same, or nearly the same, as another word.
Look at this sentence:

*I **keep** making the same mistake.*

In the Extra Column for the word **keep** you will find = **stay** next to paragraph 2.
This tells you that the word **keep**, in this context, means the same as **stay**.
It does not mean that you can always substitute one for the other in all the examples.

Here's another example: *She was wearing a blue **pullover**.*

In the Extra Column for the word **pullover** you will find = **jumper.**
The word **pullover** means the same as **jumper**, so they are synonyms here.

Now look at the dictionary entry for '**right 5** used for emphasis'.
Find the following examples and write the correct synonym
(which you will find in the Extra Column) for each example.

Examples	Synonyms
1 All of a sudden, right after the summer, Mother gets married.	_____
2 England's European Championship skills are in a right mess.	_____
3 He wants to see you right away.	_____
4 She was kept very busy right up to the moment of her departure.	_____

2 More Synonyms

Look at the following words and see if you can think of synonyms for them.
When you've finished, look them up in the dictionary.

Words	Synonyms	Words	Synonyms
1 air hostess	_____	7 matchless	_____
2 appalling	_____	8 muddle	_____
3 catastrophe	_____	9 occidental	_____
4 housebreaking	_____	10 practicable	_____
5 illegal	_____	11 react	_____
6 jail	_____	12 recap	_____

Antonyms

1 Antonyms

An antonym is a word which means the opposite, or nearly the opposite, of another word.
Look at this sentence:

*I'm sorry. How **careless** of me.*

In the Extra Column for the word **careless** you will find ≠ **careful** next to paragraph 1. This tells you that the word **careless** means the opposite of **careful**.

Here's another example:
*His feet were blue with **cold**.*

In the Extra Column for the word **cold** you will find ≠ **heat** next to paragraph 3. This tells you that the word **cold**, in this context, means the opposite of **heat**. It does not mean that they are opposites in all contexts.

Look at the words opposite and see if you can think of antonyms for them. When you've finished, look them up in the dictionary.

Words	Antonyms
1 ailing	_____
2 beautiful	_____
3 cheap	_____
4 cheer	_____
5 deterioration	_____
6 in focus	_____
7 fragile	_____
8 hatred	_____
9 heavily	_____
10 introvert	_____
11 lethargic	_____
12 profit	_____

2 Antonyms and Synonyms

Sometimes you will find both a synonym and an antonym in the Extra Column. Look at the following words and see if you can think of synonyms and antonyms for them. When you've finished, look them up in the dictionary.

Words	Synonyms	Antonyms
1 affluence	_____	_____
2 aggravate	_____	_____
3 aggression	_____	_____
4 boring	_____	_____
5 brave	_____	_____
6 cautious	_____	_____
7 check in	_____	_____
8 exact	_____	_____
9 flammable	_____	_____
10 impartial	_____	_____
11 roomy	_____	_____

Opposites and Compounds

1 Forming Opposites of Words

There are a number of different prefixes which are used to form words which mean the opposite, or more or less the opposite, of other words. For example, the opposite of 'possible' is **impossible**; the opposite of 'approve' is **disapprove**. You can, of course, also make an opposite meaning by using 'not'; for example, 'not possible' and 'not approve' or even 'not impossible' and 'not disapprove'.

Here are some common prefixes:

un- in- im- il- ir- dis- mis-

Using these prefixes, give the opposite of the words in the list below. Then look up the words you have made in the dictionary to check whether you are right.

Words	Opposites	Words	Opposites	Words	Opposites
1 happy	_____	8 distinct	_____	15 direct	_____
2 discreet	_____	9 tidy	_____	16 responsible	_____
3 legal	_____	10 appear	_____	17 legitimate	_____
4 reversible	_____	11 satisfied	_____	18 understand	_____
5 moral	_____	12 manage	_____	19 pleasant	_____
6 apprehension	_____	13 similar	_____	20 pleasure	_____
7 religious	_____	14 patient	_____		

2 Compounds

Which of these words can be joined together to form new words? For example, **black** and **board** can be joined together to form **blackboard**. When you've finished, check in the dictionary to see whether you are right.

1 black	bell	_blackboard_
2 snow	quake	_____
3 pan	bow	_____
4 green	way	_____
5 earth	stick	_____
6 blue	board	_____
7 rain	flake	_____
8 push	stand	_____
9 motor	suit	_____
10 lip	house	_____
11 swim	chair	_____
12 head	cake	_____

Words with Multiple Meanings 1

Many of the most common words in English have many different meanings.
This can be confusing when you know one meaning of a word and not the others.

Multiple Meanings

Complete the examples below with the words from the box. Only one word will fit in
the gaps in all three examples. When you've finished, check your answers by looking
up the headword in the dictionary. The first one has been done for you.

> right fine post deal blow mean drain fire bank mind

1 a The bushes and trees were __blowing__ in
   the wind.

   b A guard was __blowing__ his whistle.

   c Tourism was dealt a severe __blow__ by
   Hurricane Andrew.

2 a The little girls had locked themselves in upstairs
   because Mack had been _____ to
   them.

   b Managing well _____
   communicating well.

   c The red signal _____ you can shoot.

3 a There is a _____ view of the
   countryside.

   b He might be doing a spot of gardening if the
   weather is _____ .

   c She was _____ £150 and banned
   from driving for one month.

4 a I hope you don't _____ me calling in
   like this, without an appointment.

   b Jim Coulters will _____ the store
   while I'm away.

   c There was no doubt in his _____
   that the man was serious.

5 a ...30 miles of new developments on both
   _____ of the Thames.

   b I had £10,000 in the _____ .

   c ...Britain's National Police Computer, one of the
   largest data _____ in the world.

6 a You have to get eight wooden _____ ,
   and drive them into the ground.

   b Sir Peter has held several senior military
   _____ .

   c The winner will be notified by _____ .

7 a People have the _____ to read any
   type of material they wish.

   b Ahead of you on the _____ will be a
   lovely garden.

   c Clocks never told the _____ time.

8 a I am in a position to save you a good
   _____ of time.

   b Japan will have to do a _____ with
   America on rice imports.

   c They _____ in antiques.

9 a Many students were trapped by smoke and
   _____ on an upper floor.

   b They were _____ . I screamed at
   them to stop.

   c She was sent a box of chocolates along with a
   letter saying she was _____ .

10 a They were using their brooms to get the leaves
   out of the blocked _____ .

   b ... an emergency operation to _____
   blood from a punctured lung.

   c The colour _____ from his face.

Words with Multiple Meanings 2

Puns and Meanings

Many jokes, especially children's jokes, depend on puns. Read these jokes and
write down the two meanings of the words in *italics*. When you've finished,
look up the words in the dictionary to check their different meanings.

Jokes   **Meanings**

1 Why does an actor enjoy his work so much?
  Because it's all *play*.   _____

2 Who is the fastest runner in history?
  Adam - because he was the first in the human *race*.   _____

3 Why do soldiers like autumn so much?
  Because of all the *leaves*.   _____

4 Why did the banana go out with the prune?
  Because he couldn't find a *date*.   _____

5 Why is a baseball park cool?
  Because there's a *fan* in every seat.   _____

6 What happens to fruit and vegetables in autumn?
  People eat what they *can*, and *can* what they can't.   _____

7 Why didn't it take long to *wind up* the old man's estate?
  Because he only left a grandfather clock.   _____

8 Have your eyes ever been *checked*?
  No, they've always been this colour.   _____

9 Why don't you like going on ferries?
  Because they make me *cross*.   _____

10 Headmistress: I hear you *missed* school yesterday.
   Sam: Not one bit.   _____

11 Why was the banker bored?
   Because he lost *interest* in everything.   _____

12 I'd like a nice piece of bacon. And make it *lean*.
   Certainly madam, which way?   _____

13 What do sad fir trees do?
   They *pine* a lot.   _____

14 What flower is common to every country?
   The cost-of-living *rose*.   _____

Pragmatics 1

In the Extra Column in the dictionary you will often see the word **PRAGMATICS**. This is to draw your attention to the fact that this word or phrase is doing something which is not necessarily clear from just the meaning of the word or phrase.

Pragmatics refers to a person's intention in using the language. There are several types of pragmatic information given in the dictionary and the **Introduction** to the dictionary gives an example and explanation of each of them.

1 Thank You

Here are four of the explanations for **thank** which have a **PRAGMATICS** sign in the Extra Column. Match them with the examples.

Explanations

1 You use **thank you** or, in more informal English, **thanks** to express your gratitude when someone does something for you or gives you something.

2 You use **thank you** or, in more informal English, **thanks** to politely accept or refuse something that has just been offered to you.

3 You use **thank you** or, in more informal English, **thanks** to politely acknowledge what someone has said to you, especially when they have paid you a compliment or answered your question.

4 You use **thank you** or **thank you very much** in order to say firmly that you do not want someone's help or to tell them you do not like the way that they are behaving towards you.

Examples

A 'It's great to see you.'
'Thanks, same to you.'

B 'Would you like a cigarette?'
'No, thank you.'

C Thanks for the information.

D I can stir my own tea, thank you.

1	2	3	4

2 Indeed

Here are the explanations for **indeed**. They all have a **PRAGMATICS** sign in the Extra Column. Match them with the examples.

Explanations

1 You use **indeed** to confirm or agree with something that has just been said.

2 You use **indeed** to introduce a further comment or statement which strengthens the point you have already made.

3 You use **indeed** at the end of a clause to give extra force to the word 'very', or to emphasize a particular word.

4 You can use **indeed** as a way of repeating a question in order to emphasize it, especially when you do not know the answer; used in spoken English.

Examples

A The wine was very good indeed.

B 'Did you know him?'
'I did indeed.'

C 'And what do we do here?'
'What, indeed?'

D When we asked to see more we were refused. Indeed we were escorted away by men with gun

1	2	3	4

Pragmatics 2

Actually

Look at these definitions of **actually**:

1 You use **actually** to indicate that a situation exists or happened, or to emphasize that it is true or correct, especially when its existence or truth is surprising.

2 You use **actually** when you are correcting or contradicting someone.

3 You can use **actually** when you are expressing an opinion that other people might not have expected from you in a polite way.

4 You use **actually** to introduce a new topic into a conversation.

All four paragraphs have **PRAGMATICS** in the Extra Column. This is because the word **actually** is doing certain things in the language which are difficult to describe in terms of meaning alone. The four definitions are describing when you use the word **actually**, rather than just explaining its meaning. You should pay particular attention to this type of definition.

Here are some examples of **actually** taken from The Bank of English. Match them with the correct paragraph above.

Examples	Paragraph
1 No, a Dutch firm, actually. A big one.	_____
2 Actually, Dan, before I forget, she asked me to give you this.	_____
3 Do you actually encourage children to talk about divorce?	_____
4 I can't believe Dr Morgan is actually going to retire.	_____
5 I'd quite like a flat actually. It's cheaper as well.	_____
6 I didn't mean it that way actually.	_____
7 I think it's a disastrous influence actually but that's only my opinion.	_____
8 Actually, I didn't come here just to help you with the party.	_____
9 Can computers actually create language?	_____
10 Actually, in the negotiations, our experience was quite different.	_____
11 He actually died in exile, didn't he?	_____

Get

Some of the most common words in the English language are used in many different ways. As a result, the dictionary entries for these words are often long and detailed. The exercises in this section are designed to give you practice in the skills you need to use these entries efficiently.

1 Get 1

Get is a very complicated verb. There are over 40 sub-entries for **get** in the dictionary and over two pages of phrasal verbs formed with **get**! To make it easier for you to find the information you need, the entries have been divided into sections. These are shaded so they are easy to find. Here are the sections for **get**:

get 1 changing, causing, moving, or reaching
get 2 obtaining, receiving, or catching
get 3 phrases and phrasal verbs

When you want to look up a particular meaning of **get**, first check the sections to see which one you need.

Look at these examples and decide which section you would find them in. Then check in the dictionary.

	Section
1 He had been having trouble getting a hotel room.	_____
2 ...the ravishing island of Ischia, where rich Italians get away from it all.	_____
3 You don't seem to get the point.	_____
4 There's no point in getting upset.	_____
5 It was dark by the time she got home.	_____

2 Get 2 - Explanations and Examples

Match the explanations and the examples. These are all taken from **get 2**. When you've finished, check your answers in the dictionary.

Explanations

1 If you get something that you want or need, you obtain it.
2 If you get something, you receive it or are given it.
3 If you get someone or something, you go and bring them to a particular place.
4 If you get a meal, you prepare it.
5 If you get a particular result, you obtain it from some action that you take, or from a calculation or experiment.
6 If you get a particular price for something that you sell, you obtain that amount of money by selling it.
7 If you get the time or opportunity to do something, you have the time or opportunity to do it.

Examples

A I'm getting a bike for my birthday.
B Whenever I get the chance I go to Maxim's for dinner.
C Go and get your daddy for me.
D He can't get a good price for his crops.
E What do you get if you multiply six by nine?
F She was getting breakfast as usual.
G I asked him to get me some information.

1	2	3	4	5	6	7

Have

1 Have 1

Have is a very complicated verb. There are 28 sub-entries for **have** in the dictionary. To make it easier for you to find the information you need, the entries have been divided into sections. These are shaded so they are easy to find. Here are the sections for **have**:

have 1 auxiliary verb uses
have 2 used with nouns describing actions
have 3 other verb uses and phrases
have 4 modal phrases

When you want to look up a particular meaning of **have**, first check the sections to see which section you need.

Look at these examples and decide which section you would find them in. Then check in the dictionary.

	Section
1 They didn't have to pay tax.	_____
2 What have you found so far?	_____
3 Do you have any brothers or sisters?	_____
4 I'll have a think about that.	_____

2 Have 2

Have is used in combinations with a wide range of nouns, where the meaning of the combination is mostly given by the noun. People are more likely to use these combinations than a more specific verb. In the following sentences the 'have combinations' have been replaced by more specific verbs and although the sentences are grammatically correct, some of them sound a bit strange. Rewrite the sentences using a 'have combination'. For example, 'She breakfasted at 7 o'clock' is much less common than 'She had breakfast at 7 o'clock'.

1 Did you look at the shop when you were here?

_____

2 I'm going to shower.

_____

3 That Tuesday, Lorna breakfasted in her room.

_____

4 Sit down and rest.

_____

5 She walked in the park.

_____

6 We quarrelled yesterday.

_____

Take

1 Take with Nouns

Take is a verb that is used in many different ways as you can see by the amount of space it covers in the dictionary.

Read the following sentences. They do not always sound like natural English.
Rewrite each one adding the verb **take**, changing a verb into a noun, and making any other changes that are needed in the structure. For example, *He looked briefly at his notes* is more frequently expressed as *He took a brief look at his notes*.

1 He stepped towards Jack.   _____

2 She is always quick to be offended.   _____

3 I photographed him magnificently.   _____

4 Davis led in blaming the pilots.   _____

5 Let's break here for a few minutes.   _____

6 Nuns still vow poverty and celibacy and obedience.   _____

2 Take - Other Uses

Read the following sentences. Each example has had one word changed - the verb **take** has been replaced by another verb with a similar meaning. Find the verb and replace it with an appropriate form of **take**.

1 He gripped Sam by the hand.   _____

2 He removed a cigarette from the box on the table.   _____

3 By all means have a day or two to think about it.   _____

4 Don't forget to carry your umbrella.   _____

5 He brought her to Edinburgh.   _____

6 Let me have your coat.   _____

In each of these examples, one or more words can be replaced by **take**.
Rewrite the examples using **take**.

7 If we consider wealth as a whole, then women are a long way below average.

_____

8 Some people change the world - think of Gandhi, for example.

_____

9 What about Spain? It's the most immediate case.

_____

Who and Which

1 Who

Look at the entry for **who** in the dictionary. It is a pronoun that refers only to people.
Write the correct paragraph number after each of the following examples.

1 Who's that girl? _____

2 Do you know who is coming to the party? _____

3 I've got a client who has a sister in Australia. _____

4 It was too dark for him to see who it was. _____

5 They are serious people who laugh a lot. _____

6 ...men who have troubled marriages. _____

2 Who or Which?

Now compare **who** and **which** in the dictionary. What is the most important difference
between them? Are there any other differences? Now complete the following examples
with either **who** or **which**.

1 ...the man _____ came to tea.

2 _____ school do you go to?

3 _____'s that? Is it your sister?

4 We have two televisions, one of _____ is black
and white.

5 The blue car, _____ I'd seen earlier, was still
there.

6 Do you know _____ wrote this exercise?

7 And then it rained, _____ was a pity.

8 My brother, _____ is eighteen, is training to
be a hairdresser.

9 _____ of those books do you like best?

10 _____ of your teachers do you like most?

11 ...students _____ attend British universities.

3 Who and That

In which of the following sentences can **that** be substituted for **who**?

1 ...a tough little man who used to be a photographer.

2 Is that the boy who used to stay with you?

3 Who takes care of the store?

4 It wasn't me who suggested we should meet here!

5 ...a tall elegant woman from Switzerland, who spoke English.

6 I recently spoke to Dr Smith, who is a specialist in European affairs.

7 ...the girl who wants to marry you.

8 I don't know who his dentist is.

Answer Key

Section 1 – Finding Words and Phrases

Alphabetical Ordering

1 1 **couple** should be after **bread** and before **cupboard**
  2 **anemone** should be first
  3 **redistribute** should be after **rebellious** and before **redness**
  4 **missing** should be after **misshapen** and before **missionary**; **misshapen** should be after **mishap** and before **missing**
  5 **underdeveloped** should be first; **unnerve** should be after **undeveloped** and before **unreserved**; **undeserved** should be before **undeveloped**

2 1 destruction
  2 destructive
  3 disintegrate
  4 disinterested
  5 distinctive
  6 distinguished
  7 distortion
  8 distribution
  9 distributor
  10 district

Compounds

1 1 breach
  2 bread
  3 breadboard
  4 breadth
  5 breakable
  6 breakdown
  7 breakfast
  8 breakfast television
  9 breakfast time
  10 breakthrough

2 1 second best, second-best
  2 second-class, second class
  3 second cousin
  4 second-hand
  5 second language
  6 second opinion
  7 second-rate
  8 nightclub, night club
  9 nightgown
  10 nightlife, night-life
  11 nightmare
  12 night owl
  13 night-time, night time
  14 nightwatchman, night-watchman

Spelling

1 1 affected
  2 effect
  3 effect
  4 affected
  5 affects
  6 affect

2 1 a loose, b lose
  2 a principal, b principle
  3 a practise, b practice
  4 a stationary, b stationery
  5 a advice, b advise
  6 a licensed, b licence
  7 a desert, b dessert
  8 a complement, b compliment

Phrases 1

1 If someone **lives hand to mouth** or **lives from hand to mouth,** they have hardly enough food or money to live on.

2 *My heart was in my mouth when I walked into her office.*

3 *He has got to hear it from the horse's mouth. Then he can make a judgement as to whether his policy is correct or not.*

4 *The government might be obliged to put its money where its mouth is to prove its commitment.*

5 *'Oi, shut your mouth and have respect for elders', Langda said to the boy.*

6 *She was born with a silver spoon in her mouth and everything has been done for her.*

7 *The story has been passed down by word of mouth.*

8 If you say that someone **is putting words into** your **mouth** or **is putting words in** your **mouth,** you mean that they are suggesting that you mean one thing when you really mean something else or something different.

Phrases 2

1 blind, 11, turn a blind eye
2 eye, 25, keep an eye on
3 eye, 30, have your eye on
4 eye, 13, catch your eye
5 eye, 14, catch someone's eye
6 wool, 4, pull the wool over your eyes
7 eye, 18, cry your eyes out
8 feast, 6, feast your eyes on
9 eye, 17, shut your eyes to
10 black eye, black eye
11 eye, 35, the eye of the storm
12 naked, 7, the naked eye

Phrases 3

1 1 next
  2 nicely
  3 time
  4 well
  5 like
  6 do nicely
  7 is just as well
  8 time will tell
  9 the next thing I knew
  10 something like

2 1 In view of
  2 with a view to
  3 in my view
  4 on view
  5 in view
  6 in view of
  7 In my view

Phrasal Verbs

1 1 2
  2 1
  3 5, 6
  4 1
  5 break through
  6 breakable

2 1 33
  2 get through
  3 a 2 b 4 c 1 d 3
  3 pull away, pull back, pull down, pull in, pull into, pull off, pull out, pull over, pull through, pull together, pull up

Section 2 – Using the Explanations and Examples

Someone and Something

1 a
2 a
3 b
4 a
5 a and b
6 b
7 a
8 b

Word Order

1 1 She took their charity gratefully.
2 We are incomparably better off than we were a year ago.
3 They don't go out much, particularly during the winter months.
4 The film was incredibly boring.

2 1 small French
2 small green
3 wistful French
4 soft yellow
5 Huge wooden
6 white woollen
7 young Chinese
8 long unbroken
9 old pink check

Verbs

1	1 A	2	1 A
	2 A		2 A
	3 A		3 B
	4 B		4 A
	5 A		5 B
	6 C		
	7 C		
	8 C		

Collocations 1

1 1 weather, temperatures, day
2 task, prospect
3 wind, cold
4 building
5 hair
6 career, history, past
7 smell, taste
8 work

2 1 asleep
2 rain
3 success
4 rich
5 broke
6 new
7 cheap

Collocations 2

1 1 making a telephone call
2 do homework
3 made a mistake
4 set an example
5 do some shopping
6 set an example
7 do some shopping
8 made a telephone call
9 done his homework
10 made a mistake

2 1 make the beds, do the dishes
2 making mistakes, making decisions
3 do
4 make

3 1 gives
2 hold
3 gives
4 hold

Style and Usage 1

1 1 British English
2 used mainly in American English
3 used in spoken English
4 an old-fashioned word
5 a formal word
6 a legal term
7 a medical term
8 offensive
9 an informal word
10 used mainly in journalism
11 a technical term in economics
12 used in written English
13 a literary word

2 1 b
2 a
3 b
4 b

Style and Usage 2

1 British, faucet
2 American, bonnet
3 American, pushchairs
4 British, trunk
5 British, freeway
6 American, pavement
7 British, pants
8 American, petrol
9 American, lift
10 British, line
11 British, cookie
12 American, rubbish
13 a you wash the plates, etc.
b you wash your hands and face
14 a you want it to be discussed
b you decide to deal with it later
15 a the floor immediately above the one at ground level
b the floor at ground level
16 a a private school which parents have to pay for
b a school that is supported financially by the government and usually provides free education

Section 3 – Using the Grammatical Information

Parts of Speech

1 1 dictionary, information, meaning, words, grammar
2 give, gives, is shown
3 useful
4 just, also, clearly, concisely
5 about, of, in

2 1 a down: preposition
b down: verb
c down: adverb
2 a rings: noun
b rings: verb
3 a work: noun
b work: verb
4 a houses: verb
b houses: noun
5 a good: adjective
b good: noun
6 a right: adjective
b right: adverb
c right: verb
7 a round: noun
b round: adjective
c round: preposition
d round: verb
8 a well: adverb
b well: noun

Verbs 1

1 1 V to -inf
   2 V n n
   3 V n
   4 V prep/adv
   5 V with quote
   6 V pron-refl
   7 V that
   8 V n adj
   9 V n to-inf
   10 V n *into* -ing
   11 V
   12 V -ing

2 1 about   6 about
   2 to   7 for
   3 on   8 from
   4 on   9 to
   5 on   10 on
               11 in

Verbs 2

1 1 a V
     b V n
   2 a V n
     b V
   3 a V n prep/adv
     b V prep/adv
   4 a V
     b V n
   5 a V n
     b V
   6 a V prep/adv
     b V n prep/adv

2 1 a V *with* n
     b pl-n V
   2 a V *with* n
     b pl-n V
   3 a V *with* n
     b pl-n V
   4 a pl-n V
     b V *with* n
   5 a V n
     b pl-n V
   6 a V n *with* n
     b pl-n V n

Nouns 1

1 1 N-UNCOUNT
   2 N-COUNT
   3 N-VAR
   4 N-VAR
   5 N-UNCOUNT
   6 N-VAR
   7 N-COUNT

2 1 lack
   2 pain
   3 paperback

Nouns 2

1 1 N to-inf
   2 poss N
   3 adj N
   4 N n
   5 N that
   6 N *of* n
   7 N *for* n
   8 *in* N
   9 n N
   10 N *to* n

2 1 a her first, before a special
        court in Basingstoke
     b which most parents will
        find appealing
     c showing how the views of
        the two eyes overlap
     d same
   2 a humanitarian
     b theatre
     c my 1947
   3 a his
     b of the mass-produced
        automobile
     c Hong Kong's

Adjectives 1

1 1 a ADJ-GRADED
     b ADJ
   2 a ADJ
     b ADJ-GRADED
   3 a ADJ-GRADED
     b ADJ
   4 a ADJ
     b ADJ-GRADED

2 1 both
   2 ADJ n
   3 ADJ n
   4 v-link ADJ
   5 both
   6 v-link ADJ

Adjectives 2

1 1 ADJ *to* n
   2 ADJ *about* n
   3 ADJ that
   4 ADJ to-inf
   5 ADJ *of* n
   6 *it* v-link ADJ to-inf
   7 ADJ *of* n
   8 ADJ that

2 1 c   5 g
   2 h   6 d
   3 a   7 f
   4 b   8 e

Adverbs

1 1 ADV with cl
   2 ADV with v
   3 ADV adj/adv
   4 ADV -ed

2 1 ADV adv/prep
   2 ADV *about/going* to-inf
   3 ADV n
   4 ADV before v

Section 4 – Using the Phonetics

Consonants and Short Vowels

1 1 /ʒ/   2 1 /ɪ/, 5
   2 /dʒ/   2 /ʊ/, 3
   3 /j/   3 /e/, 5
   4 /tʃ/   4 /æ/, 4
   5 /ʃ/   5 /ʌ/, 4
   6 /θ/   6 /ə/, 3
   7 /ð/   7 /ɒ/, 4
   8 /ŋ/   8 /u/, 3
                   9 /i/, 3

Long Vowels and Vowel Combinations

1 1 /iː/, 3
   2 /ɔː/, 4
   3 /ɑː/, 4
   4 /ɜː/, 5
   5 /uː/, 5

2 1 /ʊə/, 3
   2 /aɪə/, 2
   3 /aʊ/, 4
   4 /aʊə/, 2
   5 /ɪə/, 3
   6 /eə/, 4
   7 /eɪ/, 4
   8 /oʊ/, 3
   9 /ɔɪ/, 3
   10 /aɪ/, 6

General Phonetic Practice

1 1 abandon
   2 August
   3 belong
   4 bound
   5 casual
   6 crowd
   7 deep
   8 fierce
   9 gentle
   10 hide
   11 innocent
   12 luxury

13 maybe
14 obstacle
15 outside
16 ozone
17 pace
18 pear
19 raw
20 risk

2 1 coat
2 beard
3 beer
4 bus
5 rough
6 water

3 1 AM, GB
2 GB, AM
3 AM, GB
4 GB, AM
5 AM, GB

Word Stress

1 1 about
2 area
3 arrive
4 banana
5 camera
6 chocolate
7 enter
8 perhaps
9 potato
10 receive

2 1 assembly line
2 heavy metal
3 name-drop
4 bad-tempered
5 high street
6 money-maker

3 1 a present
b present
2 a record
b record
3 a content
b content
4 a permit
b permit
5 a object
b object

4 1 photOgraph
2 doctOr
3 differEnt
4 rEport
5 papEr
6 secrEt
7 rElease
8 bettEr

Pronunciation, Spelling, and Meaning 1

1 1 a /wɪnd/
b /waɪnd/
2 a /baʊ/
b /boʊ/
3 a /liːd/
b /led/
4 a /roʊ/
b /raʊ/

2 I have a spell checker.
It came with my PC.
It plainly marks for my review
mistakes I cannot see.
I've run this poem through it
I'm sure you're pleased to know
It's perfect in its way
my checker told me so.

Pronunciation, Spelling, and Meaning 2

1 1 lunch
2 hungry
3 thin
4 helpless
5 circle
6 railway

2 1 right
2 ringing
3 week
4 floor
5 bare
6 sails
7 leak
8 red

Section 5 – Looking at Meaning

Synonyms

1 1 just
2 real
3 straight away
4 all the way

2 1 stewardess
2 dreadful
3 disaster
4 burglary
5 unlawful
6 prison
7 unparalleled
8 mess, confusion
9 western
10 feasible
11 respond
12 sum up, recapitulate

Antonyms

1 1 thriving
2 ugly
3 expensive, dear
4 boo, jeer
5 improvement
6 out of focus
7 sturdy
8 love
9 lightly
10 extrovert
11 energetic
12 loss

2 1 prosperity, poverty
2 worsen, alleviate
3 belligerence, gentleness
4 dull or tedious, interesting
5 courageous, cowardly
6 careful, rash
7 register, check out
8 precise, approximate
9 inflammable, non-flammable
10 neutral, biased
11 spacious, cramped

Opposites and Compounds

1 1 unhappy
2 indiscreet
3 illegal
4 irreversible
5 immoral
6 misapprehension
7 irreligious
8 indistinct
9 untidy
10 disappear
11 dissatisfied
12 mismanage
13 dissimilar
14 impatient
15 indirect
16 irresponsible
17 illegitimate
18 misunderstand
19 unpleasant
20 displeasure

2 1 blackboard
2 snowflake
3 pancake
4 greenhouse
5 earthquake
6 bluebell
7 rainbow
8 pushchair
9 motorway
10 lipstick
11 swimsuit
12 headstand

Words with Multiple Meanings 1

1 blowing, blowing, blow
2 mean, means, means
3 fine, fine, fined
4 mind, mind, mind
5 banks, bank, banks
6 posts, posts, post
7 right, right, right
8 deal, deal, deal
9 fire, firing, fired
10 drains, drain, drained

Words with Multiple Meanings 2

1 play, paragraph 1
   play, paragraph 7
2 race, paragraph 1
   human race
3 leave, paragraph 22
   leaves
4 date, paragraph 8
   date, paragraph 11
5 fan, paragraph 1
   fan, paragraph 4
6 can 1, paragraph 2
   can 2, paragraph 2
7 wind up, paragraph 2
   wind 2, paragraph 3
8 check, paragraph 1
   checked
9 cross 1, paragraph 1
   cross 2
10 miss 2, paragraph 9
   miss 2, paragraph 7
11 interest, paragraph 1
   interest, paragraph 9
12 lean, paragraph 1
   lean, paragraph 4
13 pine, paragraph 1
   pine, paragraph 2
14 rose, paragraph 1
   rose, paragraph 2

Pragmatics 1

1	1 C	2	1 B
	2 B		2 D
	3 A		3 A
	4 D		4 C

Pragmatics 2

1 2
2 4
3 1
4 1
5 1
6 2
7 3
8 4
9 1
10 2
11 1

Section 6 – Looking at Very Common Words

Get

1 1 2
  2 3
  3 2
  4 1
  5 1

2 1 G
  2 A
  3 C
  4 F
  5 E
  6 D
  7 B

Have

1 1 4
  2 1
  3 3
  4 2

2 1 have a look
  2 have a shower
  3 had breakfast
  4 have a rest
  5 had a walk
  6 had a quarrel

Take

1 1 He took a step towards Jack.
  2 She is always quick to take offence.
  3 I took a magnificent photograph/photo of him.
  4 Davis took the lead in blaming the pilots.
  5 Let's take a break here for a few minutes.
  6 Nuns still take vows of poverty and celibacy and obedience.

2 1 He took Sam by the hand.
  2 He took/took out a cigarette from the box on the table.
  3 By all means take a day or two to think about it.
  4 Don't forget to take your umbrella.
  5 He took her to Edinburgh.
  6 Let me take your coat.
  7 If we take wealth as a whole, then women are a long way below average.
  8 Some people change the world – take Gandhi, for example.
  9 Take Spain. It's the most immediate case.

Who and Which

1 1 1
  2 2
  3 3
  4 2
  5 3
  6 3

2 1 who
  2 which
  3 who
  4 which
  5 which
  6 who
  7 which
  8 who
  9 which
  10 which
  11 who

3 1, 2, 4, 7